FANtastic Franchises
HELLO KITTY FRANCHISE

Kenny Abdo

Fly!
An Imprint of Abdo Zoom
abdobooks.com

abdobooks.com

Published by Abdo Zoom, a division of ABDO, P.O. Box 398166, Minneapolis, Minnesota 55439. Copyright © 2025 by Abdo Consulting Group, Inc. International copyrights reserved in all countries. No part of this book may be reproduced in any form without written permission from the publisher. Fly!™ is a trademark and logo of Abdo Zoom.

Printed in the United States of America, North Mankato, Minnesota.
052024
092024

Photo Credits: Alamy, Everett Collection, Getty Images, Newscom, Shutterstock
Production Contributors: Kenny Abdo, Jennie Forsberg, Grace Hansen
Design Contributors: Candice Keimig, Neil Klinepier, Colleen McLaren

Library of Congress Control Number: 2023948520

Publisher's Cataloging-in-Publication Data

Names: Abdo, Kenny, author.
Title: Hello Kitty franchise / by Kenny Abdo.
Description: Minneapolis, Minnesota : Abdo Zoom, 2025 | Series: FANtastic franchises | Includes online resources and index.
Identifiers: ISBN 9781098285586 (lib. bdg.) | ISBN 9781098286286 (ebook) | ISBN 9781098286637 (Read-to-me eBook)
Subjects: LCSH: Sanrio Digital (Firm)--Juvenile literature. | Hello Kitty (Fictitious character)--Juvenile literature. | Cartoon characters--Juvenile literature. | Japan--Juvenile literature. | Branding (Marketing)--Juvenile literature. | Popular culture--Juvenile literature.
Classification: DDC 338.768--dc23

TABLE OF CONTENTS

Hello Kitty 4

Origins 6

Through the Years. 10

Fandom 20

Glossary 22

Online Resources 23

Index 24

HELLO KITTY

Seen on countless products and beloved around the world, Hello Kitty is a friend that fans greet in every language!

ORIGINS

Sanrio was a company founded in the 1960s. It first made silk, but went on to make sandals with cute cartoons on them. Founder Shintaro Tsuji asked Japanese illustrator Yuko Shimizu to bring those characters to life.

Shimizu sketched a white cat standing on two legs. She did not include a mouth, to show that Kitty spoke from the heart. Including "Hello" in the name promoted **social communication**.

THROUGH THE YEARS

Hello Kitty made her **debut** in 1974 on coin purses. Her design charmed fans young and old. Hello Kitty products flew off the shelves in Japan!

This excitement led Sanrio to open a store in California. More merchandise featuring the cute cat quickly followed. Everything from dolls to school supplies featured Hello Kitty!

Hello Kitty's popularity continued to grow worldwide. She was named children's **ambassador** to the United States by **UNICEF** in 1983!

In 1990, Sanrio Puroland opened its gates in Japan. The amusement park offers visitor's rides, parties, and parades! Hello Kitty cafes have also opened around the world.

Hello Kitty's popularity literally took off in 2005. EVA Air introduced travelers to Hello Kitty-themed airplanes. And in 2014, Hello Kitty caught a ride to space on a Japanese **satellite**!

Hello Kitty became so beloved, her own hospital opened in Taiwan in 2008. The **maternity** care center is decorated in everything Hello Kitty!

That same year, Hello Kitty was **appointed** Japan's tourism **ambassador** to China and Hong Kong. She became the first fictional character to take on such a role for Japan.

Hello Kitty is wildly popular in the fashion world. She has **collaborated** with famous brands like Converse and Sephora. In 2022, Nike **debuted** a limited-edition collection of Hello Kitty merch!

FANDOM

Fans have gotten to know Hello Kitty through all kinds of media, from comics to movies and video games. There have even been six Hello Kitty cartoon series!

Hello Kitty remains one of the biggest **icons** in the world. She has earned more than $80 billion! And it all started with one purrfect coin purse.

GLOSSARY

ambassador – anyone who is sent as a representative or messenger.

appoint – chosen for a particular job.

collaborate – to work with another person or group to do something or reach a goal.

debut – a first appearance.

icon – a person or thing that people recognize as a symbol of something and is an object of great respect and admiration.

maternity – of or relating to the period during which a woman is pregnant with and gives birth to a child.

satellite – a spacecraft that is sent into orbit around a planet or other space body to gather or send back information.

social communication – a set of verbal and nonverbal skills used to connect with others.

UNICEF – short for United Nations International Children's Emergency Fund, an agency that provides developmental and humanitarian aid to children worldwide.

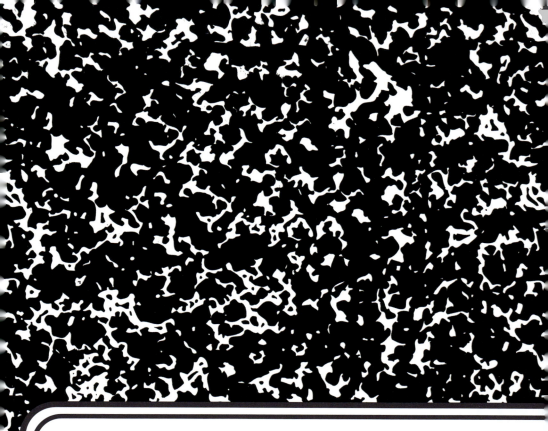

ONLINE RESOURCES

To learn more about the Hello Kitty franchise, please visit **abdobooklinks.com** or scan this QR code. These links are routinely monitored and updated to provide the most current information available.

INDEX

California 11

China 17

EVA Air 15

fans 20

fashion 10, 18

Hong Kong 17

Japan 10, 14, 15, 17

Sanrio (company) 7, 11

Sanrio Puroland 14

Shimizu, Yuko 7, 9

Taiwan 16

Tsuji, Shintaro 7

TV series 20

UNICEF 12